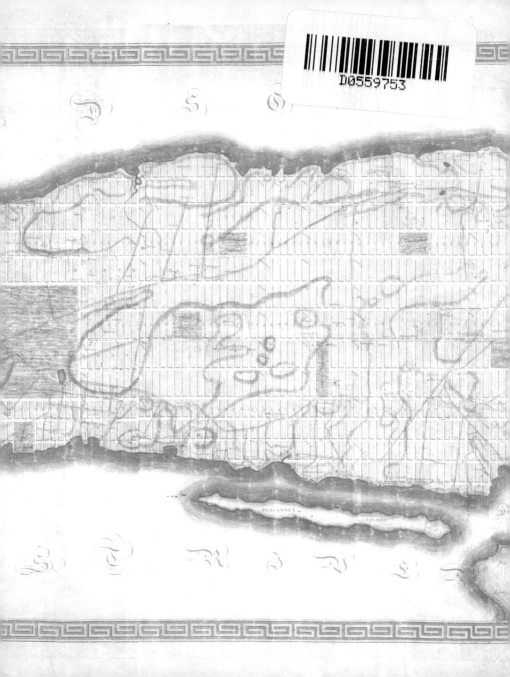

BLACKWELL'S ISLAND

On Fifth Avenue

HIGHLIGHTS OF ARCHITECTURE
AND CULTURAL HISTORY

CHARLES J. ZIGA　◆　ROBIN LANGLEY SOMMER

DOVETAIL
BOOKS

On the avenue, Fifth Avenue,
The photographers will snap us
And you'll find that you're in the rotogravure.

Oh, I could write a sonnet
About your Easter bonnet
And of the girl I'm taking to the Easter Parade.

—IRVING BERLIN
EASTER PARADE

for Ronnie
RLS

for Michael & David
CJZ

On Fifth Avenue

CONTENTS

Introduction	4
Washington Memorial Arch	6
Church of the Ascension	8
Salmagundi Club (*formerly the Irad Hawley House*)	10
Flatiron Building (*formerly the Fuller Building*)	12
Madison Square Park	14
Empire State Building	16
New York Public Library	18
Fred F. French Building	20
Charles Scribner's Sons Building	22
Rockefeller Center	24
Saks Fifth Avenue	26
St. Patrick's Cathedral	28
Cartier, Inc.	30
The University Club	32
Tiffany &. Company	34
Crown Building	36
The Plaza Hotel & Grand Army Plaza	38
Sherry Netherland Hotel	40
The Arsenal	42
Temple Emanu-El	44
The Frick Collection	46
Cultural Services of the French Embassy (*formerly the Payne Whitney residence*)	48
Metropolitan Museum of Art	50
Solomon R. Guggenheim Museum	52
Cooper-Hewitt Museum	54
Jewish Museum	56
International Center of Photography	58
Museum of the City of New York	60
Conservatory Garden, Central Park	62
Watch Tower, *Bibliography*	64

Introduction

It is altogether an extraordinary growing, swarming,
glittering, pushing, chattering, good-natured cosmopolitan place . . .

—Henry James

The first maps to show all of New York City's lots and buildings were surveyed and drawn by John F. Harrison in 1850, before the construction of Central Park made upper Fifth Avenue an increasingly desirable address. When *landscape architect* **Frederick Law Olmsted** and *architect* **Calvert Vaux** won the design competition for the 843-acre park in 1858, the way was opened to expansion along Fifth Avenue from Washington Square, as novelist Henry James knew it, to the elegant Conservatory Garden at 105th Street, near the park's northernmost reaches.

As Central Park took shape, the beauty of Olmsted and Vaux's design became apparent in the skillful integration of landscape and architectural features inspired by eighteenth-century English garden design. Picturesque glades, copses, and rocky outcroppings alternated with expanses of meadow, reflecting ponds, bridges, and countless plantings. Later, the area would be further enhanced by the electrification of the New York Central trains and the decking over of adjacent Fourth Avenue (now Park Avenue).

Prior to the mid-1800s, the area north of 59th Street had been mainly open country, dotted with squatters' shacks, and goats roamed upper Fifth Avenue. Within a few decades, palatial mansions, hotels, apartment houses, museums, and private clubs had moved steadily uptown to make "the Avenue" a byword for elegant *Beaux-Arts* architecture, culture, wealth, and fashion. Irving Berlin immortalized it in the popular song "Easter Parade," and *Leslie's Illustrated Newspaper* published sketches with such captions as "A Fifth Avenue belle superintends the packing of her Saratoga trunk in her dressing room—Preparing for the summer exodus."

Many names that resonate with a sense of the past are closely tied to Fifth Avenue. The Astors, Vanderbilts, and Whitneys of the Gilded Age entertained here on a scale never seen before, in mansions modeled on French chateaux and Venetian palaces. Financiers like J.P. Morgan and Andrew Carnegie affected the welfare of millions with their decisions. Debutantes, artists, architects, couturiers, educators, and statesmen have also left their imprint here.

This volume traces the highlights of a great American boulevard from the early nineteenth century to the present day, combining history, art, and architecture to capture a sense of the people and places whose vitality continues to enrich not only New York City, but the nation.

Washington Memorial Arch

WASHINGTON SQUARE NORTH AT FIFTH AVENUE

Gateway to Fifth Avenue

*T*his *classical* Arch of Triumph was originally built in wood and stucco in 1889 to commemorate the centennial of George Washington's first inauguration as president of the United States. Construction of the permanent marble arch began in 1892, and it was dedicated on April 30, 1895.

William Rhinelander Stewart is credited with the concept of a memorial arch and with raising the initial funds for its commission from the wealthy residents of fashionable Washington Square, which was described in Henry James's period novel of the same title.

Stanford White, *Architect,* of **McKim, Mead & White,** designed both the prototype and the present monument, which cost $128,000 to build.

The white marble triumphal arch rises at the foot of Fifth Avenue, commanding the northern entrance to Washington Square Park. It stands 77 feet high, 30 feet wide, and 10 feet deep. Like the triumphal arches of classical antiquity, it is adorned with sculptures and extensive relief carvings. Two winged figures of Victory (inset) surmount the span, and the piers bear emblems of war and peace and the American Eagle. Decorative stars and a motif of initial Ws ornament the frieze.

The sculpture on the west pier portrays *Washington in Peace,* backed by the figures of *Justice* and *Wisdom.* The inscription in the book upheld by these figures—*Exitus acta probat*—means "The end justifies the deed." **Alexander Sterling Calder**, the father of *sculptor* **Alexander Calder**, best known for his mobiles, created this sculpture. On the east pier is *Washington in War,* with *Fame* and *Valor*—the work of **Hermon A. McNeil.** Unfortuntely, air pollution has taken its toll on the marble statuary.

Washington Square Park was constructed in 1827 and soon became a wealthy residential area, as the city moved steadily uptown. New York University constructed its first building on the east side of the park in 1837, and the university remains a vital presence in the neighborhood.

N.Y.C. Historic District April 29, 1969.

Church of the Ascension

36-38 Fifth Avenue at 10th Street

Anglo-American Gothic

*T*his handsome *Gothic Revival* Episcopal church was designed by the English-born *architect* **Richard Upjohn** and completed in 1841. The influence of the British *architect* **Augustus Welby Pugin** is apparent in Upjohn's many church buildings, of which the best-known example is Trinity Church, located on Broadway at the head of Wall Street (1846).

The interior of the Church of the Ascension was remodeled in the late 1880s by **McKim, Mead & White,** *Architects.* At this time, the altar mural and stained glass by *designer* **John La Farge** were added. The altar relief is the work of **Augustus Saint-Gaudens,** *sculptor,* another major figure in what has been called the American Renaissance.

The church is a product of the ecclesiological movement in Great Britain—the artistic aspect of the Oxford Movement, which sought to revitalize the Church of England (called the Episcopal Church in the United States) by going back to its medieval roots in Roman Catholicism. *Georgian-style* Protestant church design had moved toward a spare meeting-hall format in which the pulpit was the primary focus; in medieval churches, the chancel, or area surrounding the altar, had pride of place.

Ecclesiologists favored a return to the perpendicular *Gothic* style of the fourteenth century, with its high tower and spire; clerestory bands of stained glass set high in the side-aisle walls; dramatic parapets; and a highly articulated chancel, or sanctuary. In the Church of the Ascension, the relatively shallow chancel departs to some degree from the ideal proposed in Pugin's *True Principles of Pointed or Christian Architecture* (1841), but it makes up in power and beauty for any perceived deviation from optimum depth.

N.Y.C. Historic District April 29, 1969.

Salmagundi Club

47 FIFTH AVENUE AT 11TH STREET

A Venue for the Arts

*T*his handsome *Italianate* brownstone was built in 1853 (architect unknown) as a residence for the wealthy businessman **Irad Hawley**, president of the Pennsylvania Coal Company. It is the sole survivor of the nearly solid row of brownstone mansions built of regional reddish-brown sandstone that once extended along the Avenue from Washington Square to Central Park.

In 1917 the house was purchased by the Salmagundi Club, which had been organized in 1871 to promote the arts and serve as a social center for artists. The club's name derives from Washington Irving's satirical journal of 1807-08. (The venerable New York writer is perhaps best known for "The Legend of Sleepy Hollow," "Rip Van Winkle," and other stories published as *The Sketch Book* in 1820.) Irving, who divided his time between New York City and nearby Tarrytown, is widely considered the first American man of letters.

During the mid-nineteenth century, a strong *Italianate* influence on American architecture, via English buildings and pattern books, was seen nationwide. In the country house, it was expressed in the Italian villa style, while the *Italianate townhouse* dominated urban architecture, especially on the East Coast. The Salmagundi Club is a fine example of the latter style, with its cubic form, overhanging eaves supported by paired brackets, and symmetrical façade.

The arched doorway has a heavy pediment supported by carved consoles, and full-length French windows with bracketed cornices line the main floor. The windows have been stripped of their original moldings, but the house is faithful to its period. It is typical of the many *Italianate* brownstones that once figured in the two-mile "Millionaires' Row."

N.Y.C. Landmark September 9, 1969.

Flatiron Building

175 FIFTH AVENUE AT 23RD STREET

The City's First Skyscraper

This famous triangular building derived its nickname from the wedge shape dictated by its oddly shaped lot at the intersection of Broadway and Fifth Avenue at 23rd Street. Originally, it was called the Fuller Building, for its developer. Completed in 1902, it has been compared to the prow of a great ship as well as to the homely flatiron used by housewives and laundresses at the turn of the century.

Daniel H. Burnham, *Architect,* of Chicago's highly regarded **D. H. Burnham & Company,** designed the building for this challenging site. One of its best-known predecessors is Burnham's handsome Monadnock Building in Chicago (1891). The Flatiron Building was the world's tallest when it was completed.

The 21-story tower covers the entire lot, rising 285 feet in an unbroken mass (later, setbacks on such tall buildings would be mandated by city law). The steel framework is clad with rusticated limestone and molded terracotta in the then-popular *Renaissance Revival* style. The vertical composition is based on the *classical* three-part division of a column into base, shaft, and capital. The "base" comprises the first four floors, its heavily rusticated masonry providing a solid visual anchor. The building rises another twelve stories to the ornate "capital," with its two-story arches and prominent cornice, which completes it in a highly effective manner.

A popular expression of the times originated when strong downdrafts from the building lifted young women's long skirts above their ankles, collecting crowds of admirers at the intersection. Reportedly, policemen directing traffic dispersed them with shouts of "Twenty-three skidoo!"

Eventually, the landmark building lent its name to the whole area, as commerce and fashion moved steadily up Fifth Avenue toward what is now Midtown and Uptown. The famous intersection and its environs are now popularly known as the Flatiron District.

N.Y.C. Landmark September 20, 1966.

Madison Square Park

End of "the Parade"

Originally, this historic park, opened in 1847, was part of a much larger open space designated by the city fathers in 1811 as "the Parade." When these commissioners laid out the rectilinear grid pattern for Manhattan north of Washington Square, their only provision for open space—the Parade—extended from Third to Seventh Avenues and from 23rd to 34th Streets. This area was eventually reduced to the present three-block park, named for President James Madison, between Fifth and Madison Avenues. Only the defiant diagonal of Broadway (once known as the Bloomingdale Road) cuts across the grid plan.

From the 1870s until 1900, Madison Square was the city's "downtown," dotted with the stylish department stores of Sixth Avenue (now the Avenue of the Americas), known as the "Ladies' Mile," and with expensive hostelries like the Fifth Avenue Hotel. Here was the site of the original **Madison Square Garden,** designed by *architect* **Stanford White** (1890), which occupied the square block bounded by Madison and Fourth (now Park) Avenues and 26th and 27th Streets. Today, Madison Square Park is one of the nation's great showcases of nineteenth-century sculpture, with statues of military leaders and statesmen by *sculptors* **Augustus Saint-Gaudens, Randolph Rogers, John Quincy Adams Ward,** and **George Edwin Bissell.** At this writing, a $5 million reconstruction plan is underway to restore the park to its original nineteenth-century design, with the addition of two fountains.

As fashion and its attendants moved farther uptown, the area lost its residential character and became a thriving center of commerce. Like many of the city's oldest parks, Madison Square Park was originally the centerpiece of a real-estate venture, surrounded by desirable building lots. Theodore Roosevelt was born here in 1858, in a house his family built the year after the park opened. Demolished in 1910, the four-story brownstone was replicated by Theodate Pope Riddle in 1923 on East 20th Street, where it serves as the Theodore Roosevelt Birthplace Museum.

N.Y.C. Historic District May 2, 1989.

Empire State Building

350 Fifth Avenue at 34th Street

Emblem of New York City and State

$\mathcal{W}$hen it was completed on May 31, 1931, the Empire State Building was the world's tallest skyscraper. It retained this distinction until 1972, when the twin towers of the World Trade Center surpassed it. Despite the paralyzing Great Depression, the building was completed in only eighteen months at a cost of $41 million—$19 million under budget.

Shreve, Lamb & Harmon, *Architects,* were responsible for the design.

John J. Raskob, *Developer,* conceived of and raised the funding for the Empire State Building at a time when the nation was in financial crisis.

Alfred E. Smith, *president of the Empire State Company,* had served as a popular governor of New York State for four terms and was the Democratic candidate for the presidency in 1928.

The building occupies the site of the original Waldorf-Astoria Hotel and rises 1,454 feet to the top of its television tower. Its basic components, including stone and steel spandrels and windows, were fabricated off-site and installed in assembly-line fashion. The exterior is composed of limestone, granite, nickel, aluminum, and more than 10 million bricks. Its tower rises from a five-story base to the monumental spire, which acts as a lightning conductor. As a result, the building is struck hundreds of times a year. The imposing lobby, three stories high, is finished in European marble, stainless steel, and glass in geometric patterns typical of the *Art Deco* period.

The world-famous structure was immortalized in the 1933 film *King Kong* and withstood the impact of an off-course B-25 bomber, which crashed into the 79th floor in 1945 during a heavy fog. The top thirty floors were first illuminated in 1977, when the New York Yankees won the World Series. Since then, the tower is lighted in various colors to mark seasonal holidays and special events.

N.Y.C. Landmark May 19, 1981. National Historic Landmark October 23, 1986.

New York Public Library

Reading Between the Lions

*T*his monumental building is considered one of the finest examples of *Beaux-Arts* architecture in the United States. It resulted from a merger between the Astor and Lenox Libraries and the Tilden Trust and was constructed on the former site of the Croton Aqueduct Distributing Reservoir. The library opened on May 24, 1911.

John M. Carrère and **Thomas Hastings,** *Architects,* were awarded the commission on the basis of their competition-winning design.

John Shaw Billings, *Library Director,* is credited with a major role in the planning stage, including the dimensions of the grand Main Reading Room, which measures 297 feet by 78 feet.

The symmetrical Fifth Avenue façade is constructed of white Vermont marble and is approached by a wide flight of shallow steps with expansive terraces of pink granite on either side. Three great arched bays flanked by paired Corinthian columns comprise the main entrance. The wings have two-story-high engaged columns in the same style. Between them are arched windows with sculpted lion's-mask keystones (inset). Each end of the building is completed by a bay with pediments and sculpture. Lavishly ornate inside and out, the library is replete with sculpted figures, urns, gargoyles, and friezes. Its 88 miles of bookshelves house more than 34 million volumes, manuscripts, maps, and prints, making it one of the world's five great research libraries. Thousands of people visit it on an average day.

Sculptor **Frederick MacMonnies** created the statues of *Beauty* and *Truth* on either side of the entrance. The 11-foot-high figures on the frieze, designed by **Paul Bartlett,** depict (left to right) *History, Drama, Poetry, Religion,* and *Romance.* The celebrated lions flanking the entry are the work of **Edward Clark Potter.** Originally called "Lady Astor" and "Lord Lenox," they were renamed "Patience" and "Fortitude" by Mayor Fiorello La Guardia.

National Historic Landmark 1966. N.Y.C. Landmark January 11, 1967.

Fred F. French Building

551 Fifth Avenue at 45th Street

A Monument to New York Real Estate

*T*his sparkling early *Art Deco cum Exotic Revival* building (1927) is an imposing presence, visible blocks from its busy midtown site. It was designed as headquarters for the prominent real-estate developer Fred F. French, whose firm constructed nearby Tudor City during the interwar years. This major private-enterprise venture in urban renewal comprises twelve buildings containing 3,000 apartments and a hotel in the *American Tudor* style popular in the 1920s.

H. Douglas Ives, *Chief Architect* for the Fred F. French Company, worked closely with **Sloan & Robertson,** *Architects,* who designed some of the city's finest skyscrapers, including the Chanin and Graybar Buildings.

The 38-story Fred F. French building rises in dramatic polychrome setbacks from a three-story limestone base to a soaring russet-brick shaft that culminates in a pair of faience panels depicting a rising sun flanked by griffons and bees. These symbolic bas-reliefs conceal the water tower above the triplex penthouse that crowns the building.

The intervening 32 stories, set back irregularly to conform to the recent city ordinance on high-rise buildings, are ornamented with Egyptian, Greek, and Near Eastern motifs characteristic of the *Exotic Revival* style. This theme is carried out in the bronze-and-gilt detailing of the handsome main entrances, the vaulted lobby, and the vestibule, which are richly embellished with decorative cornices, wall fixtures, and 25 paneled doors depicting Mesopotamian images associated with commerce and industry. A twentieth-century ziggurat, the Fred F. French Building is a vivid blend of historicism and emergent Modernism.

N.Y.C. Landmark March 18, 1986.

Charles Scribner's Sons Building

597 Fifth Avenue at 48th Street
A Commercial and Cultural Landmark

*A*rchitect **Ernest Flagg,** one of the "Paris men" who had studied at the Ecole des Beaux-Arts, designed this impressive building for one of the city's oldest publishers and booksellers. Completed in 1913, it incorporates elements of contemporary as well as *classical French* architecture, one of Flagg's signatures, as seen also at the "Little" Singer Building, on Broadway at Prince Street.

The three-story ground-floor bays, long the home of Scribner's Bookshop, have large show windows elegantly framed in curving cast iron, with columns of the same material, leading the eye toward the decorative mezzanine railing and other ornamental ironwork within. Flagg's distinctive use of this material is reminiscent of the work of French *architect* **Viollet-le-Duc.** The large vaulted interior has been described by architectural historian Francis Morrone as not only "the best bookshop façade in the city," but "the best retail façade of any kind."

The remainder of the façade rises gracefully through several ornamented belt courses toward the steep mansard roof. The three-bay midsection is the focal point, while the flanking end bays are decorated in a more restrained style. Central windows below the top of the building have rounded arches that delineate the corniced top story.

At the base of the mansard are two obelisks used to great effect and a two-story dormer framed by figures in relief that uphold the entablature and pediment, which is crowned by an acroterion—a large carved ornament. Like many of the "Paris men," Flagg combined Greek and Renaissance elements in his work. This was the second building designed by the architect for Charles Scribner's Sons and incorporates many of the features he used for the original downtown building.

N.Y.C. Landmark March 23, 1982.

Rockefeller Center

The City Within a City

*T*his extensive *Art Deco*-style complex is the world's largest privately owned business and entertainment center. The original nucleus comprised 14 buildings on 12 acres of land and was the first development for which skyscrapers were designed as a group. Initially, the site was to include a venue for New York's Metropolitan Opera House, but after the stock-market crash of 1929, the Metropolitan Opera withdrew from the project. In order to avoid financial disaster, the focus of Rockefeller Center shifted toward a mixed business development. Built between 1931 and 1939, the complex replaced more than 200 smaller buildings in the midtown area and employed more than 225,000 people during the Great Depression.

John D. Rockefeller, Jr., *Developer,* was a member of one of the state's wealthiest and most prominent families, well known for their civic and philanthropic activities.

Architects **Hood, Godley & Fouilhoux; Corbett, Harrison & MacMurray;** and **Reinhard & Hofmeister** worked together to design the city's first architecturally coordinated complex.

The centerpiece of the streamlined landmark is the General Electric Building (formerly the RCA Building) at 30 Rockefeller Plaza. The slender limestone tower rises from a granite base to a height of 850 feet. Its unbroken lines of vertical windows soar between limestone and aluminum cladding for 70 stories, flanked by lower structures in the distinctive *Art Deco* style. It is this combination of high and low buildings with expansive plazas and gardens that creates the spacious grandeur of Rockefeller Center.

More than 100 murals, mosaics, and scuptures, by 39 different artists, adorn the complex. Two of the best known are *Prometheus,* in the Sunken Garden (inset), and *Atlas* in front of the International Building.

The center is also home to Radio City Music Hall, the Rainbow Room, and NBC Studios. Over the years, Rockefeller Center has expanded to include 19 buildings on 22 acres.

N.Y.C. Landmark April 23, 1985. National Historic Landmark 1987.

Saks Fifth Avenue

611 Fifth Avenue at 50th Street

Clothier **Horace Saks** showed his business and fashion acumen when he moved the business founded by his father on Herald Square to midtown Fifth Avenue during the early 1920s. The block-square *Renaissance Revival* building, designed by **Starrett & Van Vleck,** *Architects,* was an immediate success and retains its elegance to this day.

Completed in 1924, Saks Fifth Avenue is a 10-story building rising from a rusticated stone base. The rounded, or chamfered, corners on the main façade mark the visual transition to the side-street elevations. The impressive entrances bear carved spiral moldings with plain cornices above them and are flanked by expansive display windows. Detailed metal grilles front the windows that surmount the doorways.

In compliance with the city's new zoning regulation on setbacks, monitored closely by the Fifth Avenue Association which keeps a "neighborhood watch" on architecture, the top three floors comprise a series of setbacks that house the business offices and the store's popular cafe. Cornices and balustrades delineate this portion of the building, which commands a view of Rockefeller Center and other midtown landmarks.

The main façade rises from the entrance level to an architrave of Indiana limestone supported by fluted pilasters. Brick sheathing covers the upper floors, with their symmetrical rectangular windows, to the seventh-story level, where a distinct sill molding articulates a series of narrower windows with intervening roundels of stone.

Now the flagship store of a wide-ranging enterprise, Saks Fifth Avenue is traditionally crowned by fourteen American flags, which ripple above the busy neighborhood on a windy day. Its festive air is enhanced during the holiday season, when the store's famous window displays attract crowds of New Yorkers and tourists alike.

N.Y.C. Landmark December 20, 1984.

Saint Patrick's Cathedral

Irish-Americans Claim Spiritual Citizenship

The patron saint of Ireland is the namesake of this imposing cathedral—the nation's largest Roman Catholic church and the seat of the Archdiocese of New York. Irish-Americans glowed with pride when Cardinal John McCloskey dedicated the cathedral on May 25, 1879. It had been under construction for 21 years and was completed at twice the estimated cost, but it showed how far a hard-pressed immigrant population had come from the time when New York businesses posted signs reading "No Irish Need Apply."

Archbishop John Hughes, an Irish immigrant who became New York's first *Roman Catholic archbishop,* announced his plan for Saint Patrick's in 1850, describing it as a church "worthy of God...and an honor to this great city."

James Renwick, Jr., *Architect,* designed the building in the *French Gothic* style. The twin spires were not completed until 1888, and the Lady Chapel was added in 1906. Renwick's many achievements include the original Smithsonian Institution building, called "the Castle," in Washington, D.C.

The site of the cathedral was originally intended for a burial ground, but proved too rocky for that purpose. When St. Patrick's was built, it was on the outskirts of the city. Its 330-foot foliated tracery spires dominated the skyline here until the 1930s, when skyscrapers of steel and glass surpassed them in height. Built in the shape of a Latin cross, with traditional east-west orientation, the white marble church is 332 feet long and 174 feet wide, making it the world's eleventh-largest house of worship. The nave, or central seating area, is 108 feet high and 48 feet wide. Its focal point is the sanctuary, where a bronze baldachin 57 feet high frames the main altar.

Above the main entryway is a circular or rose window 26 feet in diameter. The north tower houses a chime of 19 bells, and the three bronze doors on Fifth Avenue are adorned with statues of the saints designed by **Charles Maginnis** and **John Angel** in 1949. The bas-relief detail with its crossed keys of St. Peter and bishop's mitre, is the insignia of the papacy.

N.Y.C. Landmark October 19, 1966.

Cartier, Inc.

635 FIFTH AVENUE AT 52ND STREET

A House of Gold and Gemstones

*T*his beautiful *Beaux-Arts* building was originally a residence, designed for transportation magnate **Morton F. Plant,** who developed the Florida West Coast Railroad, by *architect* **Robert W. Gibson** in 1903. **C.P.H. Gilbert,** *architect,* extended the *Italian Renaissance-style* mansion before Plant sold it to his neighbor William Kissam Vanderbilt for $1 million. Vanderbilt leased it to Cartier's, the well-known jewelers, in 1917.

The mansion was converted to commercial use by *architect* **William Welles Bosworth,** who had studied at the Ecole des Beaux-Arts and the Atelier Redon. The large pediment on the East 52nd Street façade shows where the main entrance of the house was; the entrance was moved to Fifth Avenue during the remodeling. The rusticated ground floor has square-headed display windows installed by Bosworth, while the 52nd Street façade retains it round arch.

The elegant fenestration differs on each of the upper stories. The second-story windows have engaged Ionic columns and full entablatures, while the third story displays lintels on brackets and simpler cornices. Rectangular quoins mark the corners of the building to the level of the richly ornamented frieze, with its stylized foliate carving (rinceaux). The rooftop balustrade has double rather than single balusters.

Especially noteworthy are the fluted Ionic pilasters framing the grand central bay above the original entrance. Two stories high, they have Scamozzi Ionic capitals featuring acanthus leaves and paired pendants of husks. The surmounting pediment, with its round window, has paired cornucopias that contribute to the richness of the whole. This memorable example of the grand style is a fitting venue for the world-famous house of Cartier, jewelers extraordinaire.

N.Y.C. Landmark July 14, 1970.

University Club

1 West 54th Street at Fifth Avenue

A Regal Presence on the Avenue

*A*rchitect **Charles Follen McKim**, of **McKim, Mead & White**, designed this nine-story building in the *Italian Renaissance* style. Built between 1897 and 1899, its façade is of the same pink granite as that used for the terrace of the New York Public Library. This elegant palazzo was one of the exemplars of *Classical* and *Renaissance* forms for urban architecture, which McKim, Mead & White used to such great effect.

The architect was a member of the University Club, founded in 1865 to foster literature and art. It was the only gentlemen's club in the city that required a college degree for membership at that time. Originally housed in the Jerome Mansion, at 26th Street and Madison Avenue, the club outgrew this site and purchased the Fifth Avenue property for which McKim designed the new building. It incorporates heraldic-style panels of Knoxville marble inscribed to represent the eighteen colleges and universities that the majority of members had attended. *Sculptor* **Daniel Chester French**, perhaps best known for his figure of Abraham Lincoln in the capital's Lincoln Memorial, designed these carvings.

McKim made several innovations to conform the University Club to the *Florentine palazzo* style that had been emulated for gentlemen's clubs in London during the early Victorian period, notably by Sir Charles Barry. The building appears to be lower than it is because of the horizontal banding (stringcourses) between each of its three major sections; the extensive use of rustication on both the Fifth Avenue and West 54th Street façades; and the prominent multilevel cornice line that defines the roof. The high arched windows with keystones indicate the public rooms, and the smaller square windows, the bedrooms. The ornate bronze balcony railings, reminiscent of the rich naturalistic motifs used by architect Louis Sullivan, are based on Renaissance models, as is the frieze below the cornice.

Originally, a stone balustrade surrounded the building at street level, but it was removed in 1910 when the Avenue was widened. Not until 1987 were women admitted to the club under the terms of a new city ordinance. At this writing, more than 270 American and foreign institutions of higher learning are represented in the membership.

Tiffany & Company

727 FIFTH AVENUE AT 57TH STREET

A Synonym for Opulence

*T*he world-famous jewelers established by **Charles L. Tiffany,** the father of American *designer* **Louis Comfort Tiffany** (1848–1933), moved steadily uptown from its original location at 237 Broadway. This fortress-like polished-granite façade, with its imposing *Art Deco* entrance and clock (inset), and its glittering miniature display windows, is the sixth Tiffany store, built here in 1940. The building was designed by *architects* **Cross & Cross.**

The 1958 film *Breakfast at Tiffany's,* based on the Truman Capote novella and starring the elegant Audrey Hepburn costumed by Givenchy, contributed to Tiffany's mystique as the quintessential Fifth Avenue store. Its best-known predecessor is the former **Tiffany Building** at 409 Fifth Avenue and 37th Street, designed by *architect* **Stanford White** of **McKim, Mead & White,** shortly before his death in 1906. He was shot in the rooftop restaurant of his Madison Square Garden building by Harry K. Thaw, the jealous husband of White's mistress Evelyn Nesbit, in a scandal that rocked New York and the nation. White's Tiffany Building was based on the seventeenth-century *Venetian Renaissance* Palazzo Grimaldi, modified to follow the rhythm of the steel frame supporting the stately façade.

The renowned Tiffany Studios grew out of the interior-design collaborative founded by Louis Tiffany in 1879 to market his exquisite *Art Nouveau* glass, featured in many New York residences and churches. His stained-glass windows, graceful vases, and glowing chandeliers, lamps, and tiles were commissioned by wealthy clients across the United States and won European awards for design.

Like the British designer William Morris, a founder of the Arts and Crafts movement, Tiffany also produced furniture, ceramics, textiles, wallpaper, and jewelry. His creations set a new standard for the decorative arts.

Crown Building

730 FIFTH AVENUE AT 57TH STREET

Elegance Without Ostentation

Originally known as the Heckscher Building, this was the first skyscraper built in Manhattan after the 1916 zoning resolution on setbacks. Unlike the contemporaneous Fred F. French Building, there is no sign here of radical innovations in massing as a result of the new ruling. The Crown Building is unabashedly *classical* in form, and the original *eclectic* detailing included a rooster on the rooftop water-tank enclosure—shades of the rural vernacular, now re-embraced as folk art. Recently restored, gilded, and floodlighted, the building, with its crownlike apex, remains a highly visible presence on Fifth Avenue.

Warren & Wetmore, *Architects*, designed the building and saw it to completion in 1921.

Whitney Warren, a cousin of William K. Vanderbilt II, was educated at the Ecole des Beaux-Arts and formed a partnership with attorney **Charles Wetmore** in 1896. Their first notable project was the New York Yacht Club (1899), after which they went from strength to strength, partly as a result of Whitney Warren's powerful family connections, but mainly as a result of ability. Other New York buildings in which they played a major role include Grand Central Terminal (1903-13); the original Vanderbilt Hotel (1912); the Hotel Biltmore (1914); the Italian Renaissance apartment building at 927 Fifth Avenue (1917); and the New York Central Building (1929).

Warren was very active in promoting the *Beaux-Arts* style in the United States. He helped organize the Society of Beaux-Arts Architects (1895), which became the Beaux-Arts Institute of Design in 1911. He favored the French method of training students in architectural studios, or ateliers—a method adopted by Frank Lloyd Wright at his first home/studio and expanded with the Taliesin Fellowship founded in the early 1930s. Warren also organized the annual Beaux-Arts Ball in 1913 to raise scholarship funds for Americans studying in Paris. The event was a New York institution for 24 years.

An interesting sidelight on the Crown Building's history is the fact that the Museum of Modern Art opened its first gallery here, on the twelfth floor, in November 1929.

The Plaza Hotel & Grand Army Plaza

CENTRAL PARK SOUTH & FIFTH AVENUE (WEST 59TH STREET)

The Essence of New York

*T*he regal Plaza Hotel, designed by *architect* **Henry J. Hardenbergh**, opened in October 1907 to wide acclaim. The eighteen-story *French Renaissance* landmark featured 800 rooms, five marble staircases, and a two-story ballroom, and was built at a cost of $12.5 million. Its luxurious appointments and sweeping views of Central Park and Grand Army Plaza would make it the city's grand hotel *de luxe*, frequented by socialites, statesmen, foreign dignitaries—and Eloise, the irrepressible six-year-old resident created by author Kay Thompson.

The hotel rises from a three-story marble base to a ten-story midsection of light-colored brick, capped by balustraded balconies, a massive cornice, and a five-story mansard slate roof. Two corners are rounded to form symmetrical towers. The hotel's elegant Palm Court and Oak Bar have been fashionable meeting places for almost a century.

The design of Grand Army Plaza evolved from the original plan for Central Park by *landscape architect* **Frederick Law Olmsted** and *architect* **Calvert Vaux**. The boulevard took its present form after the Art Commission of New York chose the plan submitted by **Thomas Hastings** of **Carrère and Hastings**, *Architects*, in 1912. The north end of the plaza was already marked by the splendid equestrian monument to Civil War general William Tecumseh Sherman, preceded by Winged Victory, which had been created by *sculptor* **Augustus Saint-Gaudens** in 1903. Hastings aligned the semicircular island on which the statue stands with a similar island on the south side of the plaza, for which he designed the beautiful Pulitzer Memorial Fountain (1916) in the *Italian Renaissance* style. Its bronze statue of *Pomona, Goddess of Abundance* (inset), which crowns the five concentric tiers of Hautville stone, was the work of *sculptor* **Karl Bitter.** The plaza's plantings, patterned pavements, and stone benches and stanchions are integral to the design and highlight the grand entrance to south Central Park opposite the Plaza Hotel which is usually lined with horse-drawn carriages for hire.

N.Y.C. Landmarks December 9, 1969 (Plaza Hotel), and July 23, 1974.

Sherry Netherland Hotel

781 Fifth Avenue at East 59th Street

Gold Coast Grande Dame

Schultze & Weaver, *Architects*, designed this eclectic *Beaux-Arts* hotel (1927) with a colonnaded base, a square mid-section, and a series of setbacks crowned by a tall tower with an elaborate peaked roof and finial. The building defines the beginning of residential Fifth Avenue and is, in fact, a cooperative apartment hotel with a current three-to-one ratio of permanent residents to hotel guests.

The Sherry Netherland's lobby is a study in white marble, crystal chandeliers, hand-loomed carpets, and wall friezes from a former Vanderbilt mansion. The suites are also large and luxuriously appointed, with decorative fireplaces, antique furniture, and spacious marble baths. On the ground level is the shop called *a la Vieille Russie*, which is famous for its beautiful displays of Russian decorative art and antiquities, including Fabergé eggs and icons.

Two blocks away, at 795 Fifth Avenue and 61st Street, is a sister hotel by the same architects—The Pierre, built in a restrained *Beaux-Arts* style, with shallow relief ornament. The façade has single-story wings with triple arched windows that light a large dining room. At either end are the main entrance and the entrance to the popular Cafe Pierre. Slender Doric pilasters frame the arched windows, which are flanked by square-headed windows above the two entryways. A simple frieze surmounted by a balustrade with corner urns completes this level and provides the visual platform from which the central tower section rises. This slender mansarded tower on a palazzo base, reminiscent of Cass Gilbert's United States Courthouse on Foley Square, is a counterpoint to the soaring tower of the Sherry Netherland.

The Upper East Side Historic District, originally a summer enclave for wealthy families who lived downtown, burgeoned into the city's most desirable residential and shopping area at the turn of the twentieth century. From about 1910, when the first luxury apartment buildings rose here on Fifth Avenue, developers worked successfully to maintain a harmonious sense of scale among the neighborhood's larger and smaller buildings.

N.Y.C. Historic District May 19, 1981.

The Arsenal

"To House and Protect"

When what is now Central Park was still a miasmic shantytown for squatters, New York State commissioned this fortresslike landmark to house its stores of artillery, rifles, and ammunition, which were then stored in a rickety armory on Centre Street. New York City complained to the legislature in 1849 that "If the cannon be all placed in the new Arsenal, distant four and a half miles from the present depot, they would be useless, for before the troops could march that distance to obtain them, the object of a riotous mob would be accomplished."

The powers that were in Albany overrode these objections and commissioned **Martin E. Thompson**, *Architect*, to design the building, which was completed in 1851. It resembled an English manorial fortress, with eight octagonal crenellated towers in the *medieval* style—that is, with narrow openings through which missiles or molten lead could be thrown down upon assailants. Fortunately, no such measures were ever required, and the City purchased the Arsenal from the State after present-day Central Park—some 840 acres—was acquired for about $5 million.

A rough-cut granite foundation supports the five-story brick building with round- and square-headed windows below simplified hood moldings. The *Tudor-style* towers rise a full story above the roofline and anchor the mass of the building, which is sparsely adorned except for the carved door frames surmounted by an eagle and cannon balls (inset). The Arsenal served its original purpose for less than a decade before the City converted it into the headquarters of the 11th Police Precinct. *Architect* **Richard Morris Hunt** made the alterations in 1860.

As Central Park took shape around it, the former armory housed the Municipal Weather Bureau on the top floor, while the American Museum of Natural History found its first home on the second and third floors in 1869. In 1934 the building was renovated to serve as headquarters for the New York City Department of Parks (now Parks and Recreation), which is still located here. Sturdy and serene, the old Arsenal remains a reassuring presence on the Upper East Side.

N.Y.C. Landmark October 12, 1967.

Temple Emanu-El

840 FIFTH AVENUE AT EAST 65TH STREET

"God Is With Us"

*T*his great synagogue was built on the former site of Richard Morris Hunt's mansion for Caroline Schermerhorn Astor, "the" Mrs. Astor who was the arbiter of New York society's famous Four Hundred. When the congregation of Temple Emanu-El merged with that of Temple Beth-El (whose sanctuary was then located at Fifth Avenue and 67th Street) in 1927, the way was opened for construction of the world's largest Reform synagogue, which seats 2,500 worshippers.

A consortium of architects designed the handsome, mosaic-covered limestone building in the *Romanesque* style, with *Byzantine*, *Moorish*, and *Art Deco* ornamentation. Completed in 1929, it was the work of **Robert D. Kohn**, **Charles Butler**, **Clarence Stein**, and **Mayers, Murray & Philip.** The Beth-El Chapel, which memorializes the other congregation's house of worship, was built north of the main space, set back from the Avenue.

Reform Judaism began in Germany during the eighteenth century, led by Moses Mendelssohn. It diverged from Orthodox Judaism in rejecting certain restrictions of the Mosaic Law, simplifying traditional ritual, and evolving a less exclusive attitude toward other faith communities. Many German and American Jews adhered to Reform tenets, and the city's first large congregation had commissioned *architect* **Henry Fernbach** to design its temple—**Central Synagogue**, at Lexington Avenue and 55th Street (1871–72). Fernbach drew his inspiration from the Near East to construct a building in the *neo-Moorish* style, which was widely adopted by other congregations and influenced the design of Temple Emanu-El. The beautiful and intricate Moorish and Byzantine ornamentations center upon naturalistic and geometric forms, as well as symbolic representations of such Divine attributes as light and generativity. Temple Emanu-El's designers combined these elements with contemporaneous *Art Deco* features to construct a house of worship that is awe inspiring, but not overpowering. Its congregation remains a vital force in the community today.

N.Y.C. Historic District May 19, 1981.

The Frick Collection

I EAST 70TH STREET ON FIFTH AVENUE

Priceless Artworks in a Classical Setting

Many New Yorkers favor this *French Classical* mansion-turned-museum above all others, and it is, in fact, one of the nation's finest examples of the style. The original building was the work of *architect* **Thomas Hastings**, of **Carrère & Hastings**, whose partner, John Merven Carrère, died in 1911, two years before the mansion was designed for Pittsburgh tycoon **Henry Clay Frick**. Having made his fortune in coal and coke, Frick moved to New York when his companies merged with the United States Steel Corporation. The residence was completed in 1914.

The building bears the imprint of the later French Classic period of *Louis XVI*, as interpreted by the Ecole de Beaux Arts. Elegant Ionic pilasters form a rhythmic counterpoint on the façade of Indiana limestone, and the vases on the terrace steps recall the graceful urns used by Carrère & Hastings along the portico of the incomparable New York Public Library. Sculpture plays a prominent role on the Fifth Avenue façade and above the entrance on East 70th Street. *Sculptor* **Sherry Edmundson Fry**, who studied in Paris, designed the carvings.

In 1931 the house was converted into a museum by *architect* **John Russell Pope,** who created the Frick Art Reference Library. The addition made on 70th Street by *architect* **John Barrington Bayley**, a founder and first president of Classical America, was completed in 1977. Its fidelity to the original structure bears out the confidence shown by the trustees of the Frick Collection in this outstanding Classical architect, who ensured that the limestone for the single-story wing came from the same quarry that provided the original masonry. The result is a seamless garment that some critics consider the city's finest work of architecture since World War II.

Integral to the design of the addition is the courtyard garden, the work of English *landscape architect* **Russell Page**. Its highlight is a large pool with water lilies, and the north and east sides are walled by stone removed from the original building when the addition was made. The terrace garden was designed by *landscape architect* **Richard K. Webel**. The elegant wrought-iron fences are especially noteworthy.

N.Y.C. Landmark March 20, 1973.

Cultural Services of the French Embassy

972 FIFTH AVENUE AT EAST 78TH STREET

An International Venue

*T*his distinguished five-story town house was designed as a residence for **Payne** and **Helen Hay Whitney** by **McKim, Mead and White,** *Architects.* Their mastery of the *Italian Renaissance* style is apparent in the graceful curve of the façade, constructed of elaborately carved light-grey granite (a material seldom used because of its hardness).

Prominent entablatures define each story, and the carvings include wave molding above the ground floor; classical cherubs in the spandrels of the arched parlor-floor windows (inset), which are framed by Ionic pilasters; and lions' heads on the paired brackets supporting the deep cornice line of the tiled roof.

During a major restoration in 1987, a stained-glass window designed for the house by artist **John La Farge** was rediscovered.

Built between 1902 and 1906, the house reflects the wealth and taste of its original owners, from the imposing double doorway framed in white marble to the Renaissance detailing of the upper stories, with their Corinthian pilasters and rich carvings in low relief. Payne Whitney was a prominent financier and philanthropist whose passion for thoroughbred racehorses was met by extensive stables on Long Island and in Kentucky. He received the land from his uncle, Oliver Payne (who was instrumental in establishing the Cornell University Medical College). Helen Hay Whitney was a daughter of statesman John Hay, who served as secretary of state under Presidents William McKinley and Theodore Roosevelt. A poet and a notable patroness of the arts, she lived here until her death in 1944.

In 1952 the mansion began its new life as a division of the French Embassy, providing Cultural Services through departments including Artistic; Audio-visual; University, Languages, and Education; and information on studies in France. The Cultural Counselor and Deputy Cultural Counselor have their offices here.

N.Y.C. Landmark September 15, 1970.

Metropolitan Museum of Art

80TH TO 84TH STREETS

The Hemisphere's Largest Art Museum

*T*he imposing Metropolitan Museum of Art houses one of the world's most comprehensive collections, comprising more than 3 million works from the ancient, classical, medieval, and modern eras. From its *Gothic Revival* origins in the 1870s to its recent glass-walled additions, the building reflects the major architectural styles of more than a century. The spectacular permanent galleries of Greek art opened in 1999.

Architects **Calvert Vaux** and **Jacob Wrey Mould** designed the original *Gothic Revival* building, which faced Central Park, where Vaux's work is so apparent and on which Mould, an English architect, had served as an associate. The arcaded central portion of the museum's west façade is the only visible remnant of the original structure, constructed between 1874 and 1880.

Richard Morris Hunt, *Architect*, designed the monumental *Beaux-Arts* Fifth Avenue façade, which changed the building's orientation, in 1895. Called "the dean of American architecture," he was also responsible for the museum's pavilion and Grand Hall. Three great arches at the main entrance are flanked by pairs of Corinthian columns that support massive blocks of stone intended for sculptures (inset), for which monies never became available. **Richard Howland Hunt** served as *Construction Architect* after his father's death.

The museum commissioned *Architects* **McKim, Mead & White** to design the *Classical* north and south wings on Fifth Avenue, added in 1906. Their restrained elegance complemented Hunt's work to make the building an architectural masterpiece. Handsome glass-walled additions have been made by the firm of **Roche, Dinkeloo & Associates**, *Architects*, since 1975.

Two of the city's landmark buildings have been incorporated into the museum: the façade of the old Assay Office building from Wall Street (1823) is part of the American Wing; and the pediment of the Madison Square Presbyterian Church, built in 1906, is part of the Museum Library façade.

N.Y.C. Landmark June 9, 1967. Interior Landmark November 15, 1977.

Solomon R. Guggenheim Museum

1071 Fifth Avenue at 88th Street

"Let Each Man Exercise the Art He Knows."

The Guggenheim Museum is one of the city's most unique—and controversial—buildings. It opened in October 1959 after sixteen years of design and construction changes to accommodate the city's Department of Building Codes, the museum's director, and public outcry. Its organic spiral form is a radical departure from the traditional Fifth Avenue array of aligned rectangular buildings facing Central Park. Critic John Canaday called it "a war between architecture and painting." Others called it "a masterpiece."

Solomon R. Guggenheim, who made a fortune in copper, established the foundation that bears his name for his collection of non-objective art. Originally, he had focused on the Old Masters, but **Baroness Hilla Rebay**, *First Director of the Museum*, was instrumental in turning his attention to abstract art and in creating the present collection. It was she who prevailed in the selection of **Frank Lloyd Wright**, *Architect*, to design the building. A paramount force in *Modern* architecture, Wright established headquarters in the Plaza Hotel from which to work on the commission, one of the last major projects of his seventy-year career and his only building in New York City.

After the death of Solomon R. Guggenheim in 1949, completion of the museum was facilitated by the efforts of **Harry Guggenheim**, the Foundation's new president, and **James J. Sweeney**, the museum's second director.

The building is constructed of cream-colored reinforced concrete. The main gallery—an expanding spiral—is attached to the administration building, a smaller circular structure, by a concrete slab. Artworks are displayed along a quarter-mile-long ramp that spirals 92 feet up to a domed skylight. The permanent collection, housed in small galleries off the ramp, includes works by Paul Klee, Wassily Kandinsky, Marc Chagall, Robert Delaunay, and Fernand Leger. Wright intended natural lighting from the glazing that rings the outer wall, and from the skylight. Alterations to this plan were made during the 1980s, but the main gallery has since been restored to Wright's original design. The addition to the east was made by *Architects* **Gwathmey Siegel & Associates** in 1992.

N.Y.C. Landmark August 14, 1990.

Cooper-Hewitt Museum

2 EAST 91ST STREET AT FIFTH AVENUE

The Smithsonian's National Museum of Design

*T*his national museum was originally the home of iron-and-steel magnate **Andrew Carnegie**, a native of Scotland who grew up in Pittsburgh, Pennsylvania, where he made his fortune. He spent his latter years in New York as a philanthropist whose name survives in many foundations dedicated to education and world peace. Carnegie provided some $4.5 million for more than 1,600 public libraries in the United States alone.

The mansion was designed in the *Georgian Eclectic* style by *Architects* **Babb, Cook & Willard** and built between 1899 and 1902. It combines dark-red brick with bold trim of Indiana limestone, and has a modillioned roof cornice surmounted by a balustrade. One of Manhattan's last freestanding houses, the sixty-four-room mansion was built far uptown, with room for a large garden filled with flowering trees, vines, and shrubs.

In 1853 New York industrialist and philanthropist **Peter Cooper** had established the **Cooper-Union for the Advancement of Science and Art**, which opened in 1859, offering tuition-free education in art, architecture, and engineering. From the outset, Cooper envisioned a complementary museum, but his plans were delayed for almost fifty years. Then three of his granddaughters—Amy, Eleanor, and Sarah Hewitt—founded the **Cooper-Union Museum for the Arts of Decoration** (1897). It was modeled upon the Musée des Arts Decoratífs in Paris and what is now London's Victoria and Albert Museum, and the Hewitt sisters collected textiles, laces, prints, drawings, and decorative objects of the highest quality. However, the museum was in financial straits by 1963, and the collections were transferred to the **Smithsonian Institution**. The Carnegie Corporation donated the landmark mansion on upper Fifth Avenue, with its adjacent townhouse, and the buildings were converted into a museum complex, which reopened in 1976. Since then, another contiguous townhouse has been acquired, and major reconstruction has unified the disparate buildings into a cultural center that is the pride of the Carnegie Hill neighborhood and a national resource with a wide range of exhibitions. At this writing, the Cooper-Hewitt is creating the National Design Awards to honor individuals and corporations for their enlightened commitment to good design.

N.Y.C. Landmark February 19, 1974.

The Jewish Museum

1109 FIFTH AVENUE AT EAST 92ND STREET

A Beaux-Arts Mansion of Distinguished Lineage

This stately home was commissioned by **Felix Moritz Warburg** of the great banking family of Hamburg, Germany. Rather than join the family firm of M.M. Warburg & Company, he went to work in Frankfurt, where he met and married the American heiress Frieda Schiff, the daughter of Jacob H. Schiff. He became a partner in his father-in-law's firm, Kuhn, Loeb & Company, and assumed responsibility for the family philanthropies as well. Warburg founded the Federation of Jewish Philanthropies of New York. His house was completed between 1906 and 1908.

Architect **Charles P.H. Gilbert** designed what is now the Jewish Museum in the late *French Gothic* style. Its graceful curving façade recalls the houses of Jacques Coeur, in Bourges, and the Palace of Justice in Rouen, rendered freely in the style used by Richard Morris Hunt's residence for William Kissam Vanderbilt, which stood at the northwest corner of Fifth Avenue and West 52nd Street. Today, its nearest architectural relative is the Ukrainian Institute at East 79th Street.

The fenestration is especially noteworthy in its variety, from the three-centered arched windows of the second floor to the central window on the third floor, which has a depressed three-centered arch like that of the entrance. In the three dormers that crown the façade, the arches are segmental. The Gothic note is emphasized by the projections, or hood molds, over the windows, and the distinctively French roofline, with its gabled dormers and delicate metal finials.

Not fully visible from street level are the steeply pitched slate roofs, the detail of the pinnacled stone gables surrounding them, and the sixth story, with its small copper dormers. Distinctive bays and balconies enrich the effect of the Indiana-limestone façade, and many of the rooms have been preserved as they were during the Warburgs' tenure here.

N.Y.C. Landmark November 24, 1981.

International Center of Photography

1130 Fifth Avenue at East 94th Street

Neoclassical Symmetry

*T*his tasteful example of the *English Georgian* style with *Federal* touches was designed by the influential firm of **Delano & Aldrich**, *Architects*, for New York diplomat, financier, and publisher **Willard D. Straight** and his wife **Dorothy Whitney**, daughter of the Wall Street financier **William C. Whitney**. The couple entertained a wide circle of friends and dignitaries, and it was here that they founded *The New Republic.*

The architects chose red brick in a Flemish bond pattern, and marble rather than limestone trim, to execute this commission in the understated style for which they are known. It is seen also in their Greenwich House (Greenwich Village), the headquarters of the Russian Orthodox Church Outside of Russia (Park Avenue and East 93rd Street), and the private houses later occupied by St. David School at 12 East 89th Street. The Straights were also aware of their designs for the Knickerbocker and Colony Clubs.

The ground-floor windows are small, and the entryway, with its engaged Tuscan columns, is relatively modest. In the *Georgian* manner, the emphasis is on the second story, with its full-length windows and pedimented central window framed in stone. The round windows between the frieze and cornice lines are characteristic of Delano & Aldrich, who used a similar row of octagonal windows in their building for the Council of Foreign Relations. *Chief architect* William A. Delano recalled the Straight house fondly in his memoirs, where he wrote: "If I do say so, it's a well-planned and lovely house; once inside it seems much larger than it is."

The Straight family occupied the house until 1927. Its second owner, Judge Elbert H. Gary, died soon after he purchased it, and it became the home of Mrs. Harrison Williams, who entertained in a style reminiscent of the previous century, as described by the *New York Mirror* in 1840, "holding agreeable soirées and coteries, where the time imperceptibly glides on over the strains of choicest melody in the intervals of literary conversation."

In 1953 the National Audubon Society acquired the house as its headquarters, and in 1974 it was purchased by the newly established International Center of Photography, which has preserved and maintained the building in admirable style.

N.Y.C. Landmark May 15, 1968.

Museum of the City of New York

1220-1227 Fifth Avenue at 103rd Street

An Outstanding Urban Cultural Center

*F*ounded in 1923 to foster appreciation for the history and culture of a unique city, the Museum of the City of New York had its first home in the **Archibald Gracie Mansion** (now the mayor's residence), overlooking the East River in Carl Schurz Park, at East End Avenue and East 88th Street.

Within a decade, the museum needed a new building, and more than $2 million was raised from prominent New Yorkers including **John D. Rockefeller Jr.** and **Edward S. Harkness.** A design competition was held, and **Joseph H. Freedlander**, *Architect*, was chosen for his plan, which took form between 1929 and 1930.

The five-story *Georgian Colonial* design is an elegant example of this symmetrical style, built of red brick and marble. Its U-shaped plan encompasses a landscaped garden forecourt and a formal approach through a balustraded terrace. The junction of the main building and the flanking wings is delineated by marble quoins, and the projecting four-story façade has four Ionic columns supporting a pediment that bears the City shield. *Sculptor* **Adolph A. Weinman** designed the bronze statues of *Alexander Hamilton* and *De Witt Clinton* in the niches facing Central Park.

New Yorkers were enthusiastic about the new museum when it opened to the public on January 11, 1932. It was the nation's first museum of urban history, inspired by the Parisian Musée Carnavalet, and presented a fascinating array of costumes, silver, furniture, antique toys, maps and prints, period rooms, ship models, portraits, and much more.

One of the museum's first multimedia exhibitions included a Revolutionary War musket, New York's last surviving horsecar (1850), and Opera Box Number 28, rescued from the 1966 demolition of the old Metropolitan Opera House. Its ongoing $36 million restoration has enhanced its value as one of the world's major museums of urban history and culture.

N.Y.C. Landmark January 24, 1967.

Conservatory Garden, Central Park

ENTRANCE AT FIFTH AVENUE AND 105TH STREET

A Beautiful Coda to the Work of Olmsted and Vaux

*T*his three-part formal garden was originally the work of *Parks Commissioner* **Robert Moses** and *landscape architect* **Thomas Price**, who carried it out as a Works Progress Administration project in 1936, during the Great Depression. From 1899 until 1934, this area just northeast of the Croton Reservoir was the site of huge conservatories with prohibitive maintenance costs. In his usual decisive—and often controversial—style, Robert Moses had them torn down and replaced by this six-acre expanse comprising three elegant formal gardens in various styles. In subsequent years, the Conservatory Garden fell into a state of neglect, but it has been faithfully restored and even enhanced by the **Central Park Conservancy**.

The **Central Garden**, in the classic *Italianate* mode, has a spacious lawn bordered by yew hedges and allées of crab-apple trees. It frames a view of the large Conservatory Fountain, backed by a semicircular pergola wreathed in flowering wisteria. The *French-style* **North Garden** (right) follows a classical bedding-out plan whereby great numbers of similar plants are massed in elaborate floral patterns. Here is the spirited **Untermeyer Fountain**, the work of *sculptor* **Walter Schott**. Architectural historian Francis Morrone observes that "This wonderful fountain ranks with Matisse's great painting *Dance* (1909), at the Museum of Modern Art, as an expression of pure joyous abandon." Some 20,000 tulips bloom in the huge circular bed surrounding it each spring, and thousands of chrysanthemums sound the note of fall color.

The **South Garden**, which combines brilliant perennial beds and wildflowers, was restored during the early 1980s by *garden designer* **Lynden B. Miller**, who also rescued Bryant Park from near oblivion. It is a sterling example of the contemporary *American mixed border*. Access to the Conservatory Garden is through beautiful wrought-iron gates that once graced the midtown Fifth Avenue mansion of Cornelius Vanderbilt II (inset).

National Historic Landmark 1935. N.Y.C. Scenic Landmark April 16, 1974.

Watch Tower

The last of the city's fire watch towers (1855), attributed to *architect* **James Bogardus,** stands in Marcus Garvey Park (formerly Mount Morris Park), at the northernmost end of Fifth Avenue.

SELECTED BIBLIOGRAPHY

Diamonstein, Barbaralee. *The Landmarks of New York II.*

Goldstone, Harmon H., and Martha Dalrymple.
History Preserved: A Guide to New York City Landmarks and Historic Districts.

Kouwenhoven, John A.
The Columbia Historical Portrait of New York: An Essay in Graphic History.

Morrone, Francis. *The Architectural Guidebook to New York City.*

Reed, Henry Hope. *Beaux-Arts Architecture in New York: A Photographic Guide.*

Willensky, Elliot, and Norval White. *AIA Guide to New York City.*

Copyright © 2000, DoveTail Books
Design copyright © 2000, Ziga Design
Photography copyright © 2000 by Charles J. Ziga

Produced by DoveTail Books.
www.newyorklandmarks.com

ISBN 1-889461-03-2

Printed and bound in China

2 4 6 8 9 7 5 3 1

Scale of One Mile.